I0469760

Printed by Createspace, Amazon

If you would like further information about Elite Virtual Team or
other Click Convert Sell Ltd products & services email:
hello@clickconvertsell.com

Lucie Marchelot Shukla, author
The Outsourcing Game Plan: Grow Your Business With Virtual
Teams

ISBN-13:978-1516852963
ISBN-10:1516852966

CONTENTS

PART ONE:
Get Ready to Grow

PART TWO:
How to Prepare Your Business for Virtual Team Members

PART THREE:
The Outsourcing Game Plan

PART FOUR:
Fast, Effective Implementation of Your Outsourcing Game Plan

PART ONE:
Get Ready to Grow

You are about to join the ranks of the world's most successful businesses. Your name and your company can be counted alongside thousands of other growing enterprises, from startups operating on a shoestring budget to Fortune 100 companies that employ tens of thousands of people all over the globe. How? By learning to leverage outsourcing as a tool to scale up your business.

What is outsourcing?

Simply stated, outsourcing is a method of recruiting globally-based workers to manage projects and complete tasks for your business. By tapping into this ever-growing pool of "virtual talent," you give your company the opportunity to recruit talent to which you otherwise would not have access. What a boom for your business! Outsourcing, when properly managed, can be a useful tool to help you leverage your time and better manage your other resources.

Who is outsourcing for?

Contrary to popular belief, outsourcing is not just for tech companies or online businesses. Whether you own a brick and mortar business with on-site employees or are a solopreneur operating a home-based online business, you can hire virtual team members to do tasks such as bookkeeping, fulfilling customer orders, calling prospects and managing your inbox.

Beyond administrative work, virtual team members can perform more specialised tasks that you or your in-house team many not have the time or the skill set to complete.

Solopreneurs

If you are a solopreneur, you are in a good position to quickly grow your business with outsourcing. As a solopreneur, you can probably relate to the concept of having more projects to complete than time in which to complete them. It's great to be in demand, but it's also lots of hard work. Outsourcing can play an important part in helping you regain control of your time.

When you can delegate tasks you do not absolutely have to do yourself, you recapture time and energy to focus on building your business. You have the opportunity to redirect your time and talent so you can do those things which directly and immediately generate income. Outsourcing also provides you with the opportunity to add workers with specialised skills to your team. You can offer a wider range of high-value products and services and increase your brand's value to the market.

Businesses with on-site employees

Business owners who already have employees can benefit from adding a virtual team to work in tandem with their on-site team. Use your in-house team to complete the tasks that need to be done on-site like working directly with new customers, restocking products or solving problems for your existing clientele. Add a virtual team to automate the tasks that don't have to be done in-house. Plus you give your business the added advantage of functioning around the clock.

Let's say you own a dental clinic and you have an on-site team made up of superstars. While they may be great at their jobs, they still may not have the skill set to manage your social media marketing or create high-value multimedia content for your website, even on a part-time basis.

It is true that in most cases, the highest use for your on-site team is going to be centred around client-facing tasks that help improve customer experiences. Your on-site team members will be serving and following up with existing patients and answering inquiries from future patients. Those project that must be done, but that fall outside the scope of your on-site team's abilities - like marketing and online brand management - are the perfect tasks to outsource to virtual team members.

My peer group started using Filipino virtual assistants, and it was something I'd had in my mind for the last four, five years until I recruited my first one through Elite Virtual Team. From a cost perspective, it was very effective because I could get more bang for my buck. Plus, researching it, it turned out their educational system is very good, they are highly motivated and you get a lot of value.

In my business, a lot of our back office stuff and lead

If you have got a sales and marketing function to your business, which every business has, then these and your back office can be outsourced easily. If you sit down and list how many things can be done remotely in your business you will be amazed at the number of things that can be outsourced, mainly thanks to the Internet. It would be foolish for any brick and mortar company to think they can't benefit from that revolution.

I wouldn't say it was easy; there are, of course, a number of challenges when outsourcing for the first time. But if you are willing to work through these challenges then the benefits are far greater than the time and effort it takes.

Diana, the VA you (Elite Virtual Team) found me, who is an absolute star and has been part of our team for five months, has been documenting every single process within the sales and marketing functions. So now the processes are refined and we are hiring a bigger team, which makes the recruitment and training process much quicker and effective.

The biggest issue with working with VAs is making sure they don't just say "yes" and don't understand it. You need to be prepared to put in the time to teach and train people, otherwise you are wasting time and money.

- Paull Newsome,
Director at Proactive Trading Ltd,
Sales & Marketing at County Flat Roofing,
United Kingdom

Just about any task you imagine can be delegated to a skilled virtual team member. So as long as the task can be completed remotely and communicated using an Internet connection, you can organise, assign, monitor and pay for the work right online.

Outsourcing is on the rise

The Financial Times estimated the value of the outsourcing industry in the UK to be approximately £88bn in 2014. Driven by factors like cost reduction, service improvement, increased productivity and access to new technologies, the outsourcing industry has doubled in value since 2010.

Outsourcing is on the rise. There are currently more than 150 virtual job boards and marketplaces where you can find and recruit talent online. Not only are there more companies hiring virtual talent to increase productivity and profitability, but more skilled workers and trained professionals are entering the virtual workforce as a way to insert more flexibility into their work lives. The following quote from two of our virtual team members provides keen insight into the value virtual talent places on being able to work remotely:

Working towards the fulfilment of a good career in the business world is challenging. This challenge led me to work, choosing the online world of virtual assistants, while studying to get my college degree.

Now that I am married, have my college degree and am working towards my MBA/ME degree, being a Virtual Assistant is all that I need to be. The feeling of being committed to a work and life balance makes it a dream come true for me! I work from home and I can oversee the daily home chores and seeing my kids any time I want to see them, while working on tasks for clients. It's a fulfilling journey of new daily learning, character building and culture exploration.

- Karen Hobi-Wong, Legazpi City, Philippines

I am a remote worker for Click Convert Sell, employed as the General Manager. Being a remote worker means that I work my own hours and I can work from anywhere as long as there's internet connection.

My previous job was a in a company office in London with strict hours and a long daily commute. I had an accident this year that meant I could not work and lost my job.

However the joy of Click Convert Sell being a virtual office meant that I could work, I could do my work and have time for the physio appointments.

Both are very different working arenas. Being a remote worker means that you have to be a self-starter and have the discipline to get your work done. As you're not seen in the office you have to 'be seen' through your work. Therefore as a result I find my productivity levels are higher.

In an office there are so many excuses not to do the work, and perhaps a lack of responsibility.

Communication is key when working virtually. You have to communicate more proactively, better and more than you think is enough to make up for the physical distance. You do miss the office chat, but certainly not the office politics!

But I am not alone. The team uses online tools for work management, chatting and support. We are constantly messaging each other with new ideas etc. We also hold a weekly team meeting where we go through what we have accomplished and our issues, this shows accountability. There is no hiding behind colleagues. You have a really sense of achievement.

When working in a company office there was always someone else who would do that, that was their role.

A growing community of digital nomads

Fueling the increase in the amount of work being outsourced is a growing tribe of digital nomads. These are self-employed individuals, many of whom are web-based business owners, who have traded in their traditional 9 to 5 office location for the freedom of operating their own business and managing the business almost exclusively using mobile devices.

The Guardian reports there are 4.6 million self-employed professionals in the UK, making up a full 15% of the workforce. Many self-employed individuals are those who left larger companies and decided to put their expertise to work with their own venture. Instead of moving into their own offices, they have chosen to run home-based businesses or operate a portion of their workweek from a co-working location.

The coworking trend has made it possible for business owners to effectively and efficiently adopt part-time in-office hours without taking on the full-time responsibility of managing (and paying to have) their own office location. Entrepreneurs are looking for the convenience of being able to work while travelling and are finding co-working locations all over the globe when they're holidaying. As a result, a growing number of coworking communities and networks are popping up in the UK, across Europe, in America, different parts of Asia, and in resort locations the world over.

Why outsource?

If your business is humming along nicely, why would you want to go through the trouble of adding remote workers to your team? I can answer your question in one word: Leverage.

Small and mid-sized enterprises (SMEs) work with fewer resources and are usually on stricter budgets than large businesses. The challenge small and mid-sized businesses face on a consistent basis is finding the best and highest use for their resources; these include time, capital, key personnel, other employees, tools and opportunities.

Outsource to save money

Outsourcing allows you to delegate the smaller tasks (micro-tasks) to labourers for a fraction of what it would cost you to have one of your on-site team members complete the task. Outsourcing also lets you to find and hire technicians and certified professionals (whom you may not be able to afford to have on your team) to complete specialised tasks.

Outsource to leverage your resources

Restructuring your business so that you and your core team can direct all of your efforts toward generating revenue is a much higher use of your time and energy than filling your day with small tasks you can easily outsource.

As the owner and key driver of your company, you want to make sure you are able to focus on the doing the 20% of tasks that are bringing in the most money and delegating as many of the tasks you can that you don't absolutely have to do yourself.

If you are trying to grow your business, you have to get it to the point where its growth and profitability are no longer the direct result of your efforts working in the business. Delegate, delegate, delegate. Let your virtual team tackle the projects that are required for your business to function properly and you save your time and energy for the high-value tasks needed to help your business grow.

Identify tasks that you can delegate so that lower value tasks are done by your team freeing you up to focus on high value tasks that generate more income, by creating your own Delegation Graph.

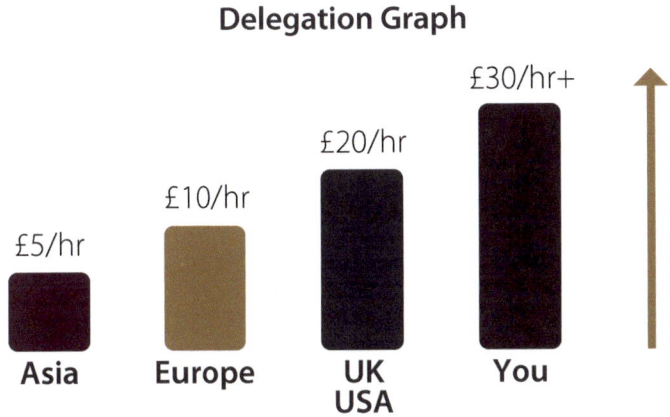

Delegation Graph

When outsourcing, think of delegating the lower value tasks to virtual assistants in other countries where you can find low cost workers like in Asia and Eastern Europe, keep the middle value ones for remote workers who speak the same language and have a similar culture to yours (United Kingdom and USA) and only work on the highest value items yourself.

Outsource to eliminate bottlenecks in your company

I have heard it said that no business can go faster than its slowest moving part. These bottlenecks - the limitations within your business operations that keep you from producing faster - are a major cause of stagnation in business. Bottlenecks keep your business from growing the way it should or the way it could. A recent survey conducted by software company Bonitasoft polled 190 professionals to find out about the inefficiencies that plague businesses. The following were ranked among the most common types of bottlenecks:

● Confusing processes
● Understaffed IT department
● Too many processes
● Colleagues missing deadlines
● Technology that is too rigid
● Not enough processes

Outsource to gain more visibility

My husband and I own two companies that are managed virtually. This model allows us to work wherever we want and arrange our schedules however we see fit. Being an entrepreneur means you need to meet lots of people, attend conferences and seminars all over the place, attend meetings and give presentations.

Very often the growth of your business depends on your ability to be seen and be available. That's impossible to do if your entire business relies on your time and talent for its survival.

I can easily communicate with my team from anywhere in the world and still be available for the weekly meetings via Skype. So, when I go home to France for the summers, I can visit my family and enjoy the weather knowing my team is working.

I love the idea of being able to travel and wander while still working and earning. With my system in place, I can even take real holidays once in a while and simply disconnect from business without worrying about things falling apart.

Outsource for 24/7 productivity

Building a team, whether on-site or off-site, helps your business increase output. Building a virtual workforce with team members from around the globe gives you the added advantage of having more productive hours.

As you begin to add team members from different countries, you will notice that many of their workdays go on during your offline hours. If you have team members in the U.S., for instance, their workday will be five to eight hours behind yours. If you have team members in the Philippines, their workday will start five to eight hours before your workday starts. Just the three of you combined can give you business 24-hour productivity. By adding workers in Asia, America, Australia and Europe for example, you can accumulate more than 24 man hours of productivity every day of the week.

How I used virtual talent to launch two businesses in two years

As a business owner, I know from experience the one thing I don't seem to have enough of is time. I have plenty of ideas. I have the drive to create successful businesses, but not nearly enough time to do them on my own.

That was the case when my husband launched our marketing agency, Click Convert Sell. We teach entrepreneurs how to create and implement profitable marketing strategies to dominate their markets using automation and outsourcing.

What an exciting opportunity! Ultimately, we were able to accomplish in our business precisely what we wanted to accomplish. Not only that, but we got a chance to help our assistant along in her journey too. Now, you may not look at things exactly in that way, but for me, being able to say I helped someone counts as a major benefit.

Social good aside, outsourcing allows me to be more productive and enjoy increased levels of efficiency. I can structure flexible work arrangements so the things I need done tomorrow are quite literally getting done while I am enjoying dinner with my family or getting a good night's sleep. Having a team that works while I am asleep is a primary advantage of hiring remote workers. I get access to world-class talent, new technologies and more hands without having to make a huge capital investment.

Implementation

Most business owners are hesitant when first introduced to the concept of growing their businesses by adding virtual talent. If you are reading this book, I can just about guess what your primary concerns are:

- How do I find the right person?
- How do I KNOW it's the right person?
- How can I put a remote worker to work quickly?

If unresolved, the above questions are usually powerful enough to stop business owners from outsourcing even though doing so would allow them to grow their business faster. That said, I want to take a few minutes here to quickly address some of the more common concerns businesses have as they decide whether or not to add virtual team members. I will go more into these points more in-depth later in this book.

Finding a quality worker

It doesn't matter what business you are in or whether you are hiring on-site workers or remote workers; hiring is never an easy job. While you can typically make hiring decisions faster when you deal with virtual team members, that speed has a lot to do with the fact that you will not have to bring the virtual team member into the fold with your other on-site employees, so it changes the dynamics of the onboarding process.

Nevertheless, hiring a virtual team member requires the same forethought, effort and conscientious decision-making as hiring an on-site team member. The most useful tool you have in making the right hiring decision is communication. Plan your recruiting efforts so there is time to:

- Create targeted, detailed job descriptions
- Build a pool of well-qualified candidates
- Ask them the right questions
- Listen to them to glean facts as well as insights

Finding a trustworthy worker

Once you find someone, how do you know your candidate will do the work to specifications and deliver on time? The truth is you don't know. Just as on-site workers often have probationary periods, you have to be ready to offer virtual employees the same leniency.

If you have done your due diligence and you are hiring from a pool of talented professionals who take their jobs seriously, it is unlikely you will recruit someone into your organisation who simply doesn't deliver. I've found it's often the case that when a virtual employee underperforms, the problem is the fault of the employer as often as it is the fault of the virtual employee. Employers are often guilty of what I refer to as the five deadly sins of outsourcing:

1. Hiring without having a definite plan in place for what the remote worker will do from day to day
2. Having no strategy in place to monitor performance and maintain accountability
3. Having unstructured workdays with job duties that vary from day to day, and are generated by the whims of the employer
4. Expecting a virtual worker to come in and build his or her own job, job description and the infrastructure in which he or she will work
5. Having no pre-existing mission, values or goals which govern the culture of the business

Too often we minimise the value of remote workers because we pay them less. There's a pervasive psychology that says since you are not paying the same amount you would pay for an on-site employee in your country, you can afford to waste your money and waste their time.

This is a dangerous mindset to have and impractical for business growth. You cannot expect any professional to work well under those conditions.

Confidentiality

Another pressing concern many business owners have is confidentiality. In fields like wealth management, intellectual property and finance for example, confidentiality and proper rights management are the core of your business and profitability. How can you trust someone from another country with sensitive information?

The remedy here is simple. First, you must keep in mind you are dealing with professionals who have taken great care to build their own reputations and careers. They are not looking to risk their livelihood by breaching your trust. So there is no greater risk in hiring virtual team members than there is hiring local team members. In fact, when you hire local talent you are probably recruiting someone who knows your competitors and because your local team members are visible, your competitors may know them and offer them a better compensation package than they get with you. On the other hand, when you outsource to offshore talent, you are not competing in a geographic location anymore. Your remote talent is essentially hidden.

Here is a takeaway you never want to forget as it relates to your hiring practices: Strong management is crucial to your employee's success.

Communicating effectively

If you are accustomed to seeing your employees in person on a daily basis, you will have to adjust to your new normal.

It is possible to effectively manage remote workers without sacrificing productivity. Nowhere has it been proven that managing online workers is less effective than managing on-site workers. In fact, studies show that just the opposite is true. Virtual workers often trump on-site workers as it relates to productivity and meeting personal, team, and company objectives.

You will learn the importance of systems and routine. When you can create and perpetuate a culture where open communication is a constant, the systems you put in place will help you to stay abreast of how your team is progressing without you having to micromanage their every move.

I will say that for SMEs hiring virtual talent for the first time, the most pressing issue they will face beyond finding and onboarding that talent is making sure remote workers have a strong, consistent Internet connection. Online technology is how you stay in touch. You will spend quite a bit of time emailing, chatting and Skyping each other. In addition, you will likely have cloud-based project management tools that your entire team will be using, so a trustworthy Internet connection is of the utmost importance.

How to use this book

After successfully launching Click Convert Sell, my husband and I were bombarded with questions from business owners wanting to know how we were able to accomplish so much in so little time. It was then that we saw the massive opportunity in the outsourcing sector. We decided to launch Elite Virtual Team, a web-based company that matches entrepreneurs to well-qualified virtual assistants from the Philippines.

I decided to write **The Outsourcing Game Plan** as a manual to help business owners and professionals understand why and how to use outsourcing as a way to help them buy back their time and grow their business. Every strategy contained in this book is one I've tested and proven as I worked to grow my startup into a six-figure business in less than a year. I used virtual team members to help me accomplish this massive feat.

By reading this book, you are going to eliminate months of trial and error from your implementation and onboarding processes. If you apply the methods I teach, you will create the systems you need in order to give your virtual team members and your business the best chance of success.

Always remember that most of your results - whether positive or negative - are driven by the processes, procedures and systems that run your business. So do the exercises, use the strategies and prepare both yourself and your business for rapid growth.

Congratulations! Your business is about to become more productive and more profitable, and in a shorter period of time than you probably think.

PART TWO:
How to Prepare Your Business for Virtual Team Members

People start businesses for a number of reasons, but there are three reasons that seem to resonate with most business owners:

- Time freedom and flexibility
- Professional independence
- Significance

Regardless of where in the world you may be and whether you are man or woman, a college student or a retired professional, there is a very good chance that one or more of the above three reasons makes it onto your list of key motivators for starting your business.

Unfortunately, what many solopreneurs and small business owners find is all three of those lofty aspirations can get lost in the fray of actually running a business day in and day out: You trade in your desire for freedom for a series of project deadlines that make you feel like a hostage in your own business. You start the business thinking you will be your own boss, but find that instead of professional independence, you have dozens of demanding customers to whom you are now responsible. It is also common for SMEs to lose sight of their mission, value and sense of significance as they turn their focus to generating profits instead of enjoying and sharing profits. If any of these problems are plaguing your business, outsourcing may be the solution you need to pull you out from under your business and put you back on top of it.

Outsourcing and automation can work for every enterprise in one way or another. The extent to which you can outsource and automate your processes really depends on the type of business you have. If you are a professional like a speaker or doctor, you have to perform in the business in order for it to function so you will not be able to outsource as much as you would if you ran a physical or digital store where everything from inventory management to marketing to sales and follow-up can be outsourced.

For the professional, outsourcing will help you to focus solely on perfecting your craft and mastering your discipline. It is your way to make the shift from trading time for money to building a business and a brand that allow you to offer higher value products and services. The key is to use your time and energy for the things you must do. Delegate everything else.

The five key areas of your business you need to prepare for the greatest outsourcing success

I have seen large companies like JP Morgan, AT&T, and Amazon successfully incompany virtual team members into their daily operations. I know from my own experience that virtual teams can be instrumental in building a business quickly. While just about any business model can benefit from outsourcing, there are five areas that can keep your outsourcing plan from effectively serving your business: Timing, talent, culture, systems, and management.

#1 Timing

Business owners often make the mistake of bringing in virtual talent too early. They think they can add remote workers without preparing beforehand.

Always qualify the need for a new team member and identify precisely how a new virtual team member will contribute to the business.

Hiring virtual talent before you have actually done your due diligence is a surefire way to make a mess of things. Before hiring anyone into your business, whether they are on-site or remote workers, be sure to have your structure, systems, management and culture already in place.

#2 Talent

So, how can you make sure you get the right people in the right positions? I will let you in on a secret: A thorough hiring process is your best insurance for hiring the right personnel.

We tend to think hiring the wrong person is something we should guard against, but hiring is not about guarding against anyone, it's about attracting someone. You attract the right talent by having an organised business with a clear focus and a well-defined role for the new worker to play. That means building a detailed job description and taking an inventory of the daily, weekly and monthly results you expect from your online talent.

If you want to recruit talent that is a good fit for your company, you have to be clear on what you need done as well as how the new team member will be expected to complete the tasks. Before putting out a call for a new team member, you should be able to succinctly identify the following:

- What objectives does your business need to accomplish?
- What specific tasks will you outsource?

- Which skills are needed to successfully complete those tasks?
- How much experience does the new team member actually need?
- Do they need special certifications or proficiencies?
- How involved will they be in your company's day-to-day process?
- What is their overall purpose in your business?

#3 Culture

Part of onboarding new talent is helping them to understand what your company is about. What are the core beliefs and values that drive your business? If you haven't already done the work of shaping your company culture, do it. It is well worth the effort and necessary to effectively lead.

Your values and mission are the single most important metric your team will use to make decisions in your business. They shape how your team thinks and how they behave. You will use your values during the hiring process to attract like-minded people to your organisation. It will be near-impossible for you to impart values onto your virtual team if you do not have them and it is hard to model for them behaviours you do not actually display.

Your job as the leader of your business is to teach your team members how each of them support the overall mission. This way your entire team - virtual and on-site - shares in the experience of moving toward a single goal or set of goals. As you add managers and workers to your team, your managers will assume the responsibility of taking what they learn from you about your company culture and passing that knowledge on to the team members in their charge. In order to be most effective, your entire team should understand and be wholly committed to upholding company culture.

#4 Systems

Systems are important to your business and essential to building a productive virtual team. These are the standard processes and procedures you put in place to ensure your business runs smoothly. Systems are the same from day to day, and perhaps most important to your virtual team, systems can be taught and replicated.

Your systems reflect your business standards and include your rules, strategies for troubleshooting problems, checklists of tasks that get completed regularly (daily, weekly, monthly, quarterly), fulfillment practices, your hardware, and the software your team uses to track and manage projects. Systems tell your team members how to handle common situations that occur in your business in accordance with the standards you set. Systems and processes allow you to delegate tasks and position your remote team to take over the aspects of your business you will no longer perform. Take over aspects of your business you don't want and should not deal with anymore in order to grow to the next level. Finally, systems are the standard by which you measure your team's performance.

#5 Management

By far, the single most important factor that determines the success of your virtual team is how you manage your team members. It's not always easy to find the right mix of guidance and autonomy. On the one hand, you want to delegate appropriately and provide sufficient instructions to online talent. On the other hand, you don't want to fall into the trap of attempting to micromanage your team.

Micromanaging any member of your team defeats the purpose of hiring help. This is one of the reasons systems are so important to your business. With systems in place, your Project Manager has a guide by which to manage your team. You can free yourself from the working in your business and take your proper position as respected leader instead of talent manager. Focus on monitoring your team's progress instead of watching their every move. Doing so allows your team members the flexibility to work independently. As long as you see yourself as the manager, you will not be able to free yourself from working in your business and it will be difficult to reach the next level.

The three types of talent to hire

There is no shortage of work to do and no shortage of global talent. Keep this in mind as you put together your outsourcing game plan. In general, there are three types of remote workers you can hire to fulfill certain roles in your business.

Freelancers and contractors

Freelancers and contractors are typically the talent you want to hire to complete short-term projects. This includes things like building websites, developing marketing funnels, graphic design work, and writing. Think of freelancers as high-value professionals who serve multiple clients, schedule multiple projects and are essentially managing businesses of their own. Their repertoire of specialised skills are in demand and you are among their roster of clients who are willing to pay for access to their talent. Creative professionals are ideal for freelance work and creative professionals also have what I call a shelf life. In my experience, creative professionals work best when they deal with multiple clients on a per-project basis.

If you attempt to add them to your team permanently, they are excited at first, but that excitement can quickly flicker out. For creative professionals, repetition is a bit like being in a cage. They need the thrill of starting new projects, facing new challenges and stretching themselves creatively or they lose interest.

Freelancers are most effective and most creative when they can be free. You may have certain freelancers with whom you work on a regular basis, but you will contact them as needed. They are not salaried workers.

Virtual team members

Virtual team members are those who have permanent or semi-permanent part-time and full-time roles in your business. They earn a fixed rate per hour, week or month no matter what they do and are typically responsible for managing a set area of your business. Tasks like bookkeeping, answering calls, and other administrative duties are ideal for your virtual team members. We will save the designation of virtual team members for those you hire to handle your day-to-day business.

Professional services

You can also hire certified professionals like barristers and accountants on a case-by-case basis to handle issues as they arise. Cloud-based software applications (Software as a Services or SaaS) can help your automate chunks of your business and cut down on your need to actually outsource directly to professionals.

For instance, subscription-based accounting systems like Xero, Wave Accounting, QuickBooks and Intacct offer full-featured accounting solutions which almost completely eliminate the data entry aspect of bookkeeping by importing your bank statements and categorising transactions automatically through regularly scheduled updates.

If you have legal questions, there are one-off online services whereby you can access a legal professional and ask a single question for a small fee. There are also websites that allow you to pay a fee to have a legal professional assist you with copyrights, trademarks and patents.

Why I strongly recommend finding Philippines-based virtual talent

You may have noticed that I keep turning your attention back to virtual talent based in the Philippines. I have a simple motive behind this. I have found workers from the Philippines have higher professional standards.

Work ethic and expertise

In my personal experience with virtual talent from the Philippines, their norm far outranks our norm. That is, Filipino workers are more enterprising and that makes them more independent. They seem to have a better entrepreneurial instinct, if such a thing exists, and they don't take their opportunities for granted. I do not see in them the attitude of entitlement that I often see in UK workers. The attitude for many UK workers is, *"I work from Monday to Friday and I have all weekends off…. I take a break at 11:15 and not a moment after."*

Filipino workers tend to be well-educated and resourceful, with fantastic communication skills. They are knowledgeable, hardworking, loyal professionals and many of them are proficient in several distinct disciplines.

It is not unusual to find a virtual assistant who is also a published writer, or a bookkeeper who also has call centre experience.

Whereas a UK worker is not typically going to be both an executive assistant and a skilled web designer, with Filipino workers, that scenario is not at all far-fetched. You have a far better chance of hiring someone with two very valuable skill sets into your organisation by looking for virtual team members who live in the Philippines.

Pay

Workers from the Philippines are far less expensive than local workers. The minimum wage for Filipino workers starts at about £150 per month, compared to the minimum wage for a UK worker, which is a little less than £1,400 per month according to Eurostat. A skilled virtual team member from the Philippines will require an investment of £300 to £500 per month. You would pay that much per week to hire administrative support staff in the UK.

Adding a standard administrative professional from the UK to your team will cost you at least £25,000 per year, plus taxes, insurance, paid holidays and employee benefits. That can be a significant investment for small businesses and will usually make adding team members cost-prohibitive for solopreneurs. It often ends up being the case that small businesses need the additional help, but cannot afford to hire local talent.

On the other hand, you can hire an assistant from the Philippines with a comparable skill set who would fit into your organisation just as well as a local team member for as little as £3,600 per year, and you will not be responsible for any employment taxes, insurance or benefits at all.

A word to the wise: Always pay fair wages. Yes, the minimum wage for Filipino workers is low, but your goal should not be to hire someone at the minimum wage. Pay a fair wage in the beginning and a generous wage soon after you find the right candidate to ensure you are able to keep you team members satisfied. I usually start my team members with a lower base salary then grow salaries quickly based on performance. One of the many benefits of outsourcing to global talent is there are no lengthy contracts involved; you negotiate pay, off days and holidays with your virtual talent directly.

In the end, hiring a virtual team member from the Philippines will require just a fraction of what it would cost to hire UK talent. So, even if you hire one virtual team member for each key area of your business, you can get an entire army of skilled virtual talent for the price of one UK employee. You can recruit high-performers and provide them the comfort of job security for a fraction of what you would pay a domestic employee with the same skill set.

Other places to find great global talent

I recruit virtual team members for Elite Virtual Team strictly from the Philippines, but I have worked with talented professionals from a number of different places.

USA

US workers have an incredible work ethic and they are, of course, fluent in English. This is a fantastic talent pool for personal assistants, copywriters, and other positions where stellar English is an important requirement. Also, with the competitive advantage of the sterling (as of this writing, £1 = $1.55), you can hire in quality team members at an affordable rate.

Eastern Europe

I also see a massive opportunity with eastern Europe in a handful of countries in economic crisis. I have worked with providers from places like Portugal and Greece. Hard-to-find jobs have driven down the wages in these places so people often need to combine different work activities to be able to cover their cost of living.

I believe Hungary is the place to watch in outsourcing right now. Hungarians speak English and they are very good in hospitality. I recently hired a worker from Hungary to handle some of my customer-facing tasks at our London based dental practice and to do some part-time on our web-based businesses remotely from home. Their culture is quite similar to ours and believe it or not, many of the workers there have been trained by luxurious hotel chains so they understand teamwork and processes. You can re-appropriate that experience to virtual work and hire Hungarian providers for customer relations positions.

I have noticed great technical talent in other parts of Eastern Europe like Bosnia and Herzegovina, Romania, Serbia and Poland. We recruit talent in these countries for design-related projects, video animation and web development projects.

Consider these places when you are ready to outsource.

PART THREE:
The Outsourcing Game Plan

In this section, I am going to teach you the strategy I used to grow a six figure business in less than a year by leveraging virtual talent and automating my business systems. Use this section to learn and implement this plan for your own business.

Let's start with a Skills Assessment. You need to know why you are outsourcing and what skills virtual team members need to possess.

THE **OUTSOURCING** GAME PLAN

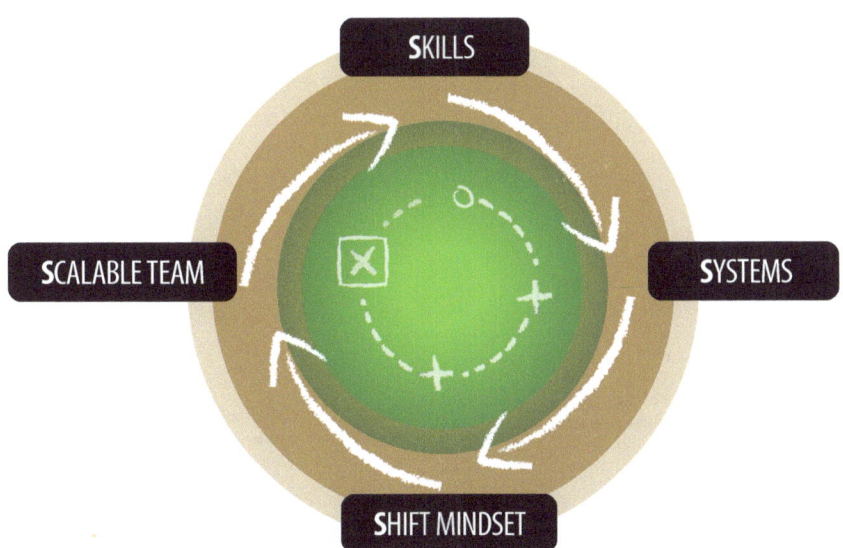

From there, create Systems to acquire and use virtual talent. Third, you need to Shift your Mindset so you do not think like a traditional employer. Then you are ready to hire someone and start building Scalable Teams. If you skip the first three steps, you greatly limit your chances of being successful.

The process of building your own virtual team takes time, strategy and of course implementation. If you need help at any point in the process, check the Virtual Team Institute where we teach you how to build your own scalable virtual team through online education programs and live workshops. Or you can hire Elite Virtual Team and we help you find top-quality virtual team members.

Let's get started.

Skills

Earlier in this book, I put forth the idea that the best way for you to find high performers is to identify the work that needs to be done in your business and use that to create a corresponding list of skills your virtual team members need to have in order to get the work done.

Identifying the skills needed is a non-negotiable part of the outsourcing process. The skills inventory is an area where you want to be very detailed. Be specific. Identify which tasks you need done and which of those tasks you will outsource.

For example, let's say you are launching a new product and you need marketing collateral for that product to ensure it has a strong online presence. Your initial to-do list and skills inventory may look like this:

- Build a landing page (web designer)
- Create social media promotion (social media management)
- Create offline promotion (graphic design, copywriting, public relations)
- Create partnerships
- Create content (writers)

On the surface, the above list may seem like a good starting point. But by providing even a little more detail about each task, you can nearly double your skills inventory and most important, get an accurate assessment of precisely what (and whom) you need.
Create your skills inventory with the intention of using it to make hires. A detailed to-do list provides you with a more in-depth understanding of precisely which skills are needed, the frequency you will need to access those skills and the specialities within each skill set (for instance, web design versus WordPress expertise) that will show up in the job description as important keywords to help you identify the right candidate for each job.

Using the list above, let's add more detail to the list using one question to get the detail we need: What sort? We need a landing page. What sort of landing page? We need writing work done. What sort of writing work? By asking that one question, you get a much better understanding of your needs.

Now, the more detailed (and more accurate) list of tasks and the skills needed to complete the tasks will look more like this:

- Build split test landing pages for each set of ads using LeadPages (marketing expertise, LeadPages expertise, sales copywriting)

- Create autoresponder series for new leads (copywriting, InfusionSoft expertise)

- Create a landing page that collects leads contact details (HTML, PSD graphic design skills and WordPress development or coding expertise, automation or auto-responder expertise, copywriting)

- Product pictures (product photography, photo editing, illustration)

- Have Google PPC ads created (sales copywriting, graphic design, PPC expertise)

- Generate clicks to website from Facebook ads, Facebook offer, share on Twitter and Linkedin too (graphic design, social media management)

- Build product pages on Facebook, LinkedIn, Google+ and Pinterest (social media expertise)

- Create content: video, blog articles (copywriting, content strategy, video animation and/or editing, graphic design)

- Build split test landing pages for each set of ads using LeadPages (marketing expertise, LeadPages expertise, sales copywriting)

- Create partnerships (researcher to put together list of partners, sales team to contact)

- Offline promotion: create sandwich board for walkins, create flyers to distribute locally, send out letters to prospects who have already opted in, create an add in the local newspaper, create a press release and contact the local press (graphic design, local flyering team, printing company, copywriter, PR)

Now you can use your complete to-do list to create a series of short job descriptions to post online in the virtual marketplace where you will be recruiting your talent.

I have designed a Digital Outsourceable Skills table, featured below. This table shows you the skills most commonly outsourced organised by difficulty, specialisation and pay. The more difficult the task, the more specialised the skill set and the more you will pay to freelancers and virtual team members who perform these tasks for you.

The type of business in which you engage may require you to have higher IT standards than another company. As such, you will be willing to pay more money for more skillful IT talent. On the other hand, if you run a successful ghostwriting firm, you may place more of an emphasis on hiring great researchers, fact-finders and writers who excel in different genres. What goes into your skills table depends on what you need for your business.

DIGITAL **OUTSOURCEABLE** SKILLS

LOW	MEDIUM	HIGH
GENERAL ADMIN		
CONTENT RESEARCH		
WEBSITE CONTENT UPLOADING		
BASIC DATA ENTRY		
PHONE AUDITING		
PERSONAL ASSISTANCE		
PROJECT MANAGEMENT		
	CUSTOMER RELATIONS	
	PHONE HANDLING	
	TELEMARKETING	
	SOCIAL MEDIA MANAGEMENT	
	BASIC ONLINE MARKETING	
	COPYWRITING	
	SEO	
	ACCOUNTING AND FINANCE	
	SALES	
	WEBMASTER	
		WEB-DESIGN
		WEB-DEVELOPEMENT
		IT
		GRAPHIC DESIGN
		LEGAL SERVICE

Overcoming "this can't be outsourced" syndrome

There will be times when you come across jobs that seem so specialised that they can't be outsourced. This is where it becomes extremely important to be proficient at reverse engineering a job duty.

I recall working with a client who wanted to outsource the position of Quantity Surveyor. Initially, I didn't know how in the world I would fill the position. None of the candidates to whom I had access had experience as a Quantity Surveyor. I solved my dilemma by doing what I told you to do - break down the job itself. I had to ask myself, "What skills does a Quantity Surveyor need? What do they need to know? What do they need to learn?" Once I shifted my focus from hiring for a job to recruiting for a series of tasks, I was able to find and interview several highly qualified remote workers from the Philippines with backgrounds in finance and accountancy.

Outsourcing is not about filling positions and passing out job titles; it's about making sure every task has an owner who is willing and able to complete that task well. So if you run into a situation where you have a position that you cannot seem to fill, break down the position into a series of tasks and micro-tasks that can be by one or more virtual assistants in minutes. Use the techniques I discussed earlier to conduct an in-depth analysis of each task. Focus on identifying what needs to be done and you will be able to find the talent you need to do it.

Perfecting your hiring process

With your skills inventory firmly in your mind, start by shaping a job description for a full-time Project Manager.

The Project Manager

The first person you hire should be your Project Manager (PM). This is the person who will serve as your right hand in your business. That person will know your business inside and out and understand what it is you want to accomplish with your business as well as everything about your daily business operations. The Project Manager is your first hire because it is the PM who will help you organise the hiring process and supervise the other virtual team members you hire.

Your PM will probably be the only generalist on your team. This person is the go-between, getting instructions and goals from you and directing the rest of your virtual team on how to help the company reach its goals. Your Project Manager can help you create workflow systems and provide you with feedback on how they are working in real-time.

You may be tempted to hire several providers at once but resist the urge. If you are not already crystal clear on what each new team member will do and how they can be of use to you on a consistent basis, you will waste time and money by adding personnel to hastily. Remember, your virtual team members provide you with ongoing support. These are full-time hires so you want to make sure you already have their responsibilities properly mapped.

Specialise

It is a good idea to hire people to focus on one specific area of your business. Refrain from hiring anyone to fulfill several roles. People are very rarely good at managing multiple roles. They will likely perform well in one area and underperform in the others.

So while you will find virtual talent that has multiple proficiencies, focus on making good use of their core strengths and fall back on their secondary talents only if you have to. Do not hire someone who will fulfill two distinctly unrelated needs (like call centre and web design). Let your people specialise. It's better for your business if you have six virtual team members and each one has his or her tasks to do rather than have one or two team members who handle everything. That's true for both on-site and online personnel.

Full-time versus part-time

When you first start with virtual team members you may want to hire someone part-time on a trial basis. If you can afford to bring someone in full-time right from the beginning, do that. The reason is simple: You want to grow your business with key team members who are committed to your business. When you hire someone on a part-time basis, that person will have multiple jobs, multiple clients, and divided attention. How can they be fully committed to their own goals, your goals and the goals of a multitude of other employers?

I have tried working with virtual talent on a part-time basis and my experience is they are not as successful as full-time employees. You want to hire in virtual team members who will be 100% committed to your business.

Personality tests

Another useful tool in the hiring process is the personality test. There are paid and free personality tests, which I will discuss more later in this book. If you are in the early stages of your hiring process and whittling down your candidate pool, you may want to use free personality tests to gauge how candidates think and how they respond. I use The Innermetrix Disc Index. It is a modern interpretation of Dr William Marston's behavioural dimensions and uncovers the four quadrants that help understand a person's behavioral preferences.

How to think like a recruiter and attract the best fit every time

Recruiters understand the one thing that outranks hard skills when it comes to hiring and retention are behavioural competencies. More than anything, a person's work personality and their disposition toward the overall company mission are key determining factors in whether or not a candidate will be a good fit for your company. More than their ability to use software and execute techniques, you need to have a good sense of how your team members will work independently and how they work collaboratively.

It's only been in the last two decades that the concept of emotional intelligence (also known as behavioural competencies or soft skills) has been widely regarded as a key leadership tool. Core competencies are defined in the Harvard University Competency Dictionary as: "... The 'things' that an individual must demonstrate to be effective in a job, role, function, task, or duty. These 'things' include job-relevant behavior (what a person says or does that results in good or poor performance), motivation (how a person feels about a job, organisation, or geographic location), and technical knowledge/skills (what a person knows/demonstrates regarding facts, technologies, a profession, procedures, a job, an organisation, etc.)."

Behaviours matter

Behavioural competencies will be useful in helping you choose the virtual team member that's right for your company. Soft skills make the difference when you are choosing between several candidates with similar technical skills. Use your job description to identify the technical skills a candidate needs to have in order to be successful with your company. Then use personality tests and a thorough interview process to help you experience first-hand a candidate's behaviours.

For virtual talent, and in fact any new team member, whether working physically or remotely in your business, **attitude is key**. I always look at how they present themselves. Have they put any thought into their email communication with me? Are their responses to my questions well-written? Are they grammatically correct, cohesive and consistent? I find when I hire in the Philippines, applicants will blindly reply to dozens and dozens of job postings, so it's helpful to me in determining the quality of talent with whom I am engaging if I know they can tell me the position for which they are being interviewed.

You should conduct live Skype interviews with any candidate you are considering for a position. When you conduct Skype interviews, how do they respond? Are they responsive, or are their responses limited to a series of one-word answers? Do they offer any ideas or add any value to the conversation? The level of responsiveness (or unresponsiveness) a candidate demonstrates during the interview can be an indicator of how future interactions with the provider may go.

I also encourage you to ask test questions. Dream up a few scenarios and ask candidates how they would handle or remedy the situations.

You may ask an applicant for search engine optimisation work how he or she would write a meta description for a particular page on your site. Or you may ask someone who is interviewing for a sales position to go through a sales call with you where you play the role of the prospect and the candidate's job is to get you to buy.

These techniques will go a long way toward helping you choose the right candidate straight away, saving you time and money and in the long run. I often have to interview dozens of people just to find one team member to add for EVT. And that's fine.

It's worth it to invest a sufficient amount of time on the front end if you can add a great worker to your team who will help you go grow your business.

Systems

Now that you know how to hire virtual team members, let's put the systems in place that will help you scale your business.

Why your business needs working systems

I alluded to this in a previous section, but I want to make sure you are clear on the importance of systems. Your business needs an effective, proven system in place before you start recruiting virtual talent. If you add your team members before you have a system in place, you will lose time and sacrifice productivity managing and instructing your team members day after day. It's better to create a workflow process and teach them that process one time. This way, you take yourself out of the business of managing their day-to-day activities. You only have to check in on them once or twice a week to monitor progress and mediate any problems that arise.

Creating a working system is the one thing that will get you out of your business. It is your pathway to go from working in your business everyday to working on your business and reserving your time, talent and energy for high-value tasks. If you fail to create systems that allow you to delegate tasks efficiently, your virtual team members will fail and you will not be able to build a scalable business. Your system will teach your team members several important things:

- How to work according to your standards

- How to manage tasks on a schedule and complete them on time

- How to deliver consistent quality in everything they do

- How to work collaboratively and maintain open lines of communication to minimise confusion, eliminate duplicate efforts and rid the work environment of stress

- How to make the best use of the resources, time and talent they have

- How they can achieve their individual goals while supporting team and company goals

I think the hardest thing for business owners to reconcile when they first start the outsourcing process is finding the time to do everything that needs to be done in order to successfully implement their outsourcing game plan. After all, part of the reasons you are outsourcing in the first place is because you need to regain control of your time. Where do you find the time to create and test a series of systems that your virtual talent can use?

If you are struggling to find the time to create your systems, create one system and hire your PM to help you create the others.

The five steps of creating an effective system

Now turn your focus to building the road map your team members need in order to support your company goals.

#1 Get experience

The first step in creating any system is to do the work yourself. If you are a solopreneur, you may already have hours, days, weeks and months of experience creating content or making phone calls or managing your own books. So you may already be uniquely qualified to teach your virtual team members what to do and how to do it to get the best results.

#2 Build a Standard Operating Procedure (SOP)

If you are delegating a task that needs to be done and you have no actual experience doing the task, seek the assistance of an expert and ask the expert to help you create a standard operating procedure that will work within the context of your business. For instance, someone who is running an online business but who does not have time to create content and write copy may hire a freelance content strategist to create the system your virtual team will actually use to create high-value multimedia content on a consistent basis.

#3 Test the system

Once you and the expert have created the standard operating procedure, go through the system a few times on your own

#4 Identify the strengths and possible weaknesses in your system

You need to be able to pinpoint the key elements that make the entire process successful. There is a difference between having a theoretical understanding of a process and understanding a process through application. Getting hands-on experience running the processes in your business gives you the advantage of perspective. When problems inevitably arise whose solutions are not listed in your handbook, having experience in the problem area will help you troubleshoot the problem. A client once told me to remedy this he asks his virtual team members to record themselves when going through the process so he can identify any barriers and refine his system.

#5 Create a training manual, graphics and checklist

Once you identify the strengths and weaknesses in your system and made any necessary changes, write down the process. You are now ready to delegate the task to a virtual team member. When you create your instruction manual or checklist, highlight the important parts, including potential barriers, hacks and the things which must be done in order for the process to work. It is also a good idea to create visually-appealing charts and graphs to provide your team members with an at-a-glance reference guide that will help them get back on track if they forget a step or get stuck somewhere along the way. This part is important.

In my own business, I went through the process of recruiting, interviewing and hiring talent for months before I decided to delegate that task. I knew that in order to create the manual explaining the process, I had to know the process well and be able to offer my PMs support in the event they ran into any issues during the hiring process.

If I were to charge one of my Project Managers with the task of adding team members without a guide to follow, I can just about guarantee their idea of a "good candidate" would not match my idea of a "good candidate." Because I went through the process many times myself, I was able to provide my PMs with detailed instructions, including what questions to ask, what to watch out for, and even how to distinguish quality emails from poor emails. I used my own experiences hiring virtual talent to create templates and checklists so my PMs at Elite Virtual Teams know exactly how to conduct an interview to recruit top talent for my clients.

They write notes beside each question and adhere to a strict rubric to make hires. We even go so far as to assign Quality Checkers who share the same culture as our clients so we can make sure we are able to properly align with our clients. Now, I have PMs who can use the training manual to find top candidates based on my standards. I never have to worry about whether my PMs are recruiting quality virtual talent and I don't have the added stress of worrying that my clients won't be satisfied because we have a system in place to ensure we can find and hire superior virtual talent.

Again, creating the systems and the instruction manuals to teach those systems may require a significant time investment on the front end, but investing 40 hours this month to create a system that will save you 240 man hours per year going forward is a worthwhile investment.

Create great systems

Do not make the rookie mistake of leaving the management of your business up to your Project Manager and your virtual team.

They are not in charge of the systems; they are in charge of completing the tasks that make your system (and thus your business) work. At the Virtual Team Institute, we help entrepreneurs create great systems that allow them to delegate efficiently and grow their business rapidly. The goal is always to create systems that make your team's success almost fail-proof and to document those systems in a way that you team can easily understand and remember. You can use tools like Skitch for visually-interesting notes, Jing for screenshots and screencasts, and Prezi for engaging presentations.

Shift Mindset

What comes to mind when you hear the word "employment?" Do you think of grey offices and fluorescent lights? Do you think of eight-hour workdays and half-hour lunch breaks? Do you think of strolling by the desks of the people who directly report to you and peeping over their shoulders for a moment or two before they realise you are there? If this is the imagery you summon when you think of business, you are due for a shift in your mindset.

The simple truth is if you do not shift your mindset, you will go into outsourcing with outdated thinking and your outsourcing game plan will fail. You will do well to remember this: As the business owner, you are in charge, but your virtual team is in control. Don't try to control them or keep them on a short leash. Give them room to be productive in accordance with your standards. Dan Sullivan, Co-Founder of Strategic Coach® often says: "Move away from being in control to being in charge and get clear on your role as the leader in your company".

Trade in your corporate mindset for the P.A.C Mindset

Productivity, Alignment and Connection (P.A.C.) are the big three when it comes to working with a virtual team. Let's talk about the three essential elements that will help you get the best from your virtual team.

P.A.C Mindset

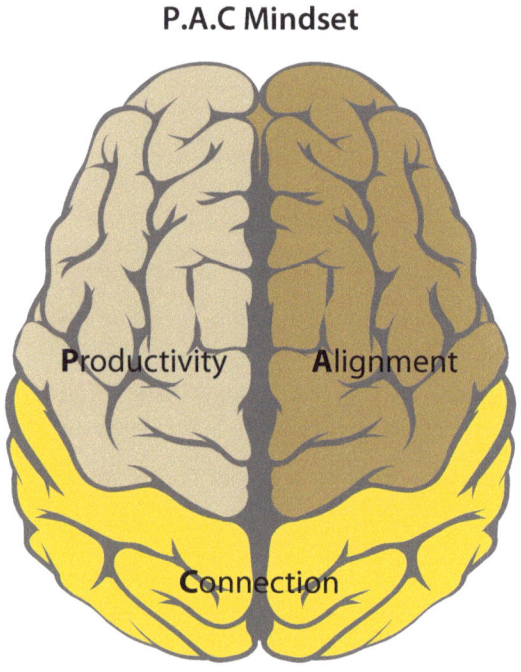

Productivity

Productivity is the bottom line in outsourcing. You will be recruiting team members who live in different time zones. Many of them will be five to twelve hours ahead of you, depending on where you are in the world. It would be counter-productive for you to attempt to manage your virtual talent in the same way you manage your on-site team. Not only will your attempts be futile, but you will reduce productivity and likely drive away your best team members.

Here's an important strategy: Abandon the Monday through Friday, 9 to 5 mindset and unlearn the traditional relationship between an employee and an employer. I truly believe that seeing your staff as equals and giving them the opportunity to grow together is a much more productive way of growing a business. Of course you have to be clear and assert yourself as the respected leader of your organisation and everybody should know that you are the one to take the risks and therefore have the last word, but you want to encourage your team to create their own jobs. Give them the chance to earn their place in the organisation. The more they produce, the more they get. Your business will not only grow faster, you will be able to delegate more and work as a member of a nicely aligned team.

Remote workers don't work remotely so they can be chained to a desk all day. The moment you put restrictions on their schedules and start demanding they be at their desks by a certain time every morning, you all but eliminate the likelihood that your team members will extend their work hours to finish pressing projects. Instead of thinking like a traditional employer, think in terms of productivity. There is only productivity; the results are what matter.

I think it's a good practice to find out from your team members why they work remotely. Ask them and listen to their answers without suppositions and without judgments. Our team member Tom relocated to Bali. He started by sharing space with other co-workers until it was time for him to settle in a private office to avoid distractions. His working arrangement works for him and it doesn't interfere with his productivity when he works with us.

You will find your team members have different reasons for working from home. Some are trying to avoid traffic and the stress of going into an office every day. Some are part-time students and want work that allows them time flexibility. Others may want to be home with small children or ailing parents.

For me, I actually work best from home. I have an office space in my home that I only use when I am working. I am most productive in my office. There have been days when I have worked comfortably for ten hours straight with no break. The space I created in my home is designed for optimal focus. There are no distractions, no co-workers coming over to distract me, no unnecessary meetings that require my time and attention. I know from experience that if I had to work in a traditional office setting, I would not be as productive. I control my own time. If I have to receive a delivery, I can. If I want to go see a friend, I do. It does not compromise my productivity.

For most virtual talent, productivity is a matter of mindset and self-motivation, not location. Team members who work in the Philippines have different reasons for wanting to work from home. Working from home may be a better option for some than working at an office in Manila, where the commute to work every morning may be a two-hour crawl along roadways in congested traffic. It's a hot, uncomfortable mess and that's before they even start their workday. Can you imagine starting every morning that way then being expected to perform at your very best? And what happens during the day as it gets closer and closer to the time when they have to go back out in that traffic to suffer through the two-hour drive back home?

When you conduct some or all of your business online, it's easy to forget that the social media profiles and email accounts you engage with on a daily basis have actual people behind them.

Make your relationship with your virtual team members professional as well as interpersonal. Find out who they are and what drives them. Ask them why they work from home. Find out what about the arrangement brings them the most joy and offers them the greatest benefit. You want to know ahead of time so you never make the mistake of infringing on their joy and minimising (or eliminating) what they perceive as the true benefits of working remotely. Then when possible, do what you can to boost that joy.

When people believe that you are for them, that you support them and care about their well-being, they are more than willing to go the extra mile for you. So while it may seem easier to be disinterested, in the long run, your disinterest is not in the best interest of your company. Apathy neither facilitates loyalty nor does it encourage a collaborative environment - two qualities you always want working between you and your virtual team members. A happy, satisfied team member is a productive team member.

> "
> *Working as a Virtual Assistant made my life happier and more flexible. I finished my law degree while working as a VA the whole time. This line of work makes my life more manageable because I get to control my time. I also need not worry about waking up early in the morning just to travel and join the morning rush to an office. I get the same value and substance. I'm learning and earning while doing what I love. It's what I call living the dream.*
>
> **- Stela Benitez, Manila, Philippines**
> "

Alignment

It is important for you to be able to not only connect you team members to each other, but to find a common ground between your team and your business. Alignment means you and your team members share in and support a single mission or vision - you understand and support their vision for their lives and they understand and support your vision for the business.

Your values and mission are important. They are important to you, they are important to your business and they are important to your team. Your values and mission are the current that move your business in a specific direction and if you have delayed identifying your values or mission, now is the time for you to get clarity in those two areas.

Your mission and value statements should resonate with your team members. Business owners often make the mistake of developing missions and values that carry no impact in the real world. They either sound like company descriptions or they end up being a jumble of words and ideas that have little to do with the way in which you get things done in the market.

Connection

A successful working relationship with globally-based talent requires alignment, the practice of gaining a clear understanding of the cultural nuances that impact how your will work together.

When you work with Filipino virtual assistants for example, you should understand they are not confrontational or culturally conditioned to take the lead. They will implement your instructions quite well.

It seems like a small thing, but if you overlook this one difference and assume you high-performing team members are what we refer to as "go-getter" you may make the mistake of giving your virtual talent too much responsibility without providing enough instruction to direct them and you may be setting your team member up to fail.

Another example of a cultural difference that can negatively impact your business is the habit Indian providers have of saying yes, often too hastily. Having worked with Indian freelancers on certain projects in the past, and more recently having been married in India, I can say that in their culture they say yes without having even listened to the question. If you do not know that going in, you can end up getting very excited about virtual workers who say "Yes, I can!" and in the end be very disappointed when you discover they can't. Always present your team members with clear expectations and provide clear examples of the results you want to see. Yes, they are skilled, yes they are capable. But you want their standards and your standards to be aligned.

Create and share your mission and values statements

Your values and mission are important. They are important to you, they are important to your business and they are important to your team. Your values and mission are the current that move your business in a specific direction and if you have delayed identifying your values or mission, now is the time for you to get clarity in those two areas.

Your mission and value statements should resonate with your team members. Business owners often make the mistake of developing missions and values that carry no impact in the real world.

They either sound like company descriptions or they end up being a jumble of words and ideas that have little to do with the way in which you get things done in the market.

Your mission statement is essentially your abbreviated strategy for succeeding in your business. It should be well-defined and clear enough to positively impact your team members. The mission makes your course of action and the general direction of the company crystal clear.

Whereas leadership is responsible for creating the mission statement, identifying the values that drive the company can be a collaborative effort between you and your team. At their core, values are just behaviours. They are specific and succinct and they dictate how you and your team will accomplish the mission.

Create a company handbook

Your mission statement and your values should be written down. They are not effective until you put them some place where you and your team can read them. Remember, their role is to govern how your business acts and what it ultimately does in the market. They should be on your company's website and they should be included in your team handbook, along with information about your company.

Unlike the instruction manuals for different processes, your company handbook should not be technical; it should be professional with an conversational flow to it. The handbook is your team's guide to how you engage online, how to engage with your clients, how to take decisions when they are on their own, how they are to interact with each other and what is the long term vision for the company.

Use your handbook as a gateway to better understand each other, instead of a rulebook that does little to build trust.

Use the handbook to tell your story. How did your company come to be? How long have you worked in your industry and how long did it take you to figure out you wanted to run your own business? Where is the business going over the next five years? Ten years? Why are you in this business? By sharing your story and helping your team to understand why and how your business operates, you help them to also understand where they fit in the process. Help them to bond with your brand. Give them a strong sense of belonging.

Assign glorifying titles and roles

Now is also a good time to tell you to be careful about how you assign titles. I tried to steer clear of the concept of bosses and employees; these delineations can have unpleasant, even hostile associations.

As an example I always discuss the job title with a team member before I assign it. I never refer to my team as employees or staff always as colleagues or team members whether with them or in my private life. The moment you think differently, you start to see them differently and ultimately you treat them differently.

I talked a bit earlier in this section of how important it is for you to see your virtual team members differently. They are talented, independent, valuable professionals who have chosen to help you grow your business. Yes, you want them to be loyal to you, but you also want to show them that you are concerned with their well-being. Show them you understand that it's not just about you. This is the whole essence of the Shift Mindset in the Outsourcing Game Plan.

Adopt a habit of making your team members feel good. Value them and their work; choose job titles that demonstrate their value. That doesn't mean you have to make up lofty titles that have no substance behind them. You and your team members are collaborators. They are helping you to reach your professional goals and you are helping them to reach their personal goals.

I know from experience how hard it is to work for a company that does not see you or care about you. I worked for a well-known corporate company in the auction industry that did not make me feel valued professionally. Millions of workers have similar experiences and worse every single day of their professional lives. No one is going to give their best to an organisation that minimises them and makes them feel unimportant.

Positively and productively review their performance by showing them what they did well. Praise them in front of the other team members or even on your social media feed. But also make sure you back your verbal praises with actual monetary rewards. Often it is the case that employers only make time to highlight an employee's mistakes. But always turning the spotlight on someone's failures does not evoke change and does not encourage long-lasting improvement. Highlight what your team members are doing right and help them correct that which is lacking.

Go the extra mile and they will go the extra mile

Talk to your team members. What are their goals? Is there a member of your team who wants to buy a house? Help him buy. Give him some extra work so he can earn a bit more every month.

Maybe he needs another £100 a month to qualify for a mortgage. Assign him a few side projects every month to help him close the gap financially and start the buying process.

I remember having a team member whose dream was to own an iPhone. So we paid her a little extra per month to help her buy one. Do you think she worked even harder for us and was even more committed when we showed her that we care about her personal goals, not just her professional performance? Of course she did! For us, it was a small price to pay to increase the satisfaction of a team member who was already a high performer.

It is your job to understand your team members' life visions and personal goals and show them (not just tell them) how they can achieve their goals working with you. So share your mission, visions and values. Make sure they understand and feel excited about what you do and they become advocates of your business. When you write the handbook, include the information that impacts your team - your story, vision, core beliefs, and goals. Let them figure out how they will help you to meet and exceed your wildest dreams then you do the same for them.

Share in the fame, share in the successes

Share in all successes. Any goals you accomplish, you did so together. You owe it to your team to recognise them privately and publicly for their hard work. As much as you may love the praises heaped on you for your great ideas, fantastic product or innovation, assume your team members want to be celebrated just as well. Nothing lowers team morale faster than working with an unappreciative company. Resist the temptation to take all the credit yourself. You cannot foster loyalty that way and you may find yourself losing some of your most valuable team members. Praise your team and reward them for their efforts. Teamwork makes the dream work.

Scalable Team

Now that the first three elements are in place for your outsourcing game plan, let's now identify how to scale your business. This step of the process can be quite complex. If you have trouble with implementation, I invite you to check out my Virtual Team Institute where I teach ambitious entrepreneurs how to implement The Outsourcing Game Plan and specifically the SUCCESS formula.

How to scale your team using the SUCCESS Formula

Use the SUCCESS Formula to build a scalable team:

Segment
Understand
Count
Communicate
Evaluate
Stimulate
Set goals

Segment

Grow your team bit by bit. You may start with one Project Manager to oversee your virtual team. As you grow your team, you will add one new team member per business unit. As you streamline your processes and start seeing better results, you will assign team members to each business unit so you have multiple team members per business unit.

Then you will be able to assign one person to each task within the unit. Roles and segmentation are an effective method of delegating tasks and measuring performance.

Consider how hotels segment and manage the massive number of team members that work in the hotel. The general manager oversees the entire operation. But there are also managers over each division within the hotel. A hotel may have 15 members on the housekeeping team, each responsible for maintaining certain areas or floors in the hotel and the housekeeping team will have a supervisor. There may be 10 team members who run the front desk 24 hours a day, and a supervisor to whom they report. The kitchen will have its own team and its own manager. Regardless of when you arrive at the hotel for check-in, you will be met by one of the 10 front desk staff members. The kitchen staff never clean the hotel and you will not find the housekeeping staff in the kitchen. Think of your business the same way.

Segmentation is the most efficient way to make optimal use of your team's time and talents. Each member gets really good and very efficient at the task to which he or she is assigned.

I use personality tests to help me determine the best use for my virtual team members. Personality tests identify their natural disposition, their tendencies and even their hidden talents. I use them to gain a deeper understanding of the areas where they can excel. I learn the types of tasks my team members need to do more and which they should do less. The three personality tests I use are StrengthsFinder, Kolbe Index, and How to Fascinate.

Assigning roles and responsibilities ensures you know what is being done and can measure the results. It also allows you to plan and scale your business accordingly.

Understand

Understand is about team culture; it is about knowing how to collaborate and how to foster an open, productive work environment that connects your online team with your offline team.

My staff and I have a document that we use whenever new members join the team. I have the new person fill out the form then I share the completed form with the entire team. This is one of many team-building rituals we use with Click Convert Sell and Elite Virtual Team. And we do it to create a sense of unity and collaboration.

You have to be careful when you add a virtual team to a business that already has on-site team members. It's easy for your on-site team members to start to feel threatened by your virtual team. So it's important that every member of your team understands his or her role and importance and that he or she has the opportunity to build positive, productive relationship with both your online and offline staff.

An easy way to help foster a sense of connection and collaboration is to have regular team meetings where you and your team members discuss personal productivity goals, their family goals and their business goals for the week, month and year. Usually, you only have to get the conversation started and your team members will find a common ground on their own. Something wonderful happens when people are allowed to share their aspirations. Bonds are created and a community forms. When your team members share their goals, make a note and follow up with them in the weeks and months to come. When they reach their goals, give them the opportunity to follow up with the team to glory in their achievement.

Another great way to help your team members connect is to host annual company events. Create at least one event per year if you can. Set aside one day a year where you can all spend time together, enjoy activities, meet the families, and get to know one another. If possible, you may even consider arranging a trip together.

In the end, it doesn't matter where they are working as long as they are well connected to you, to the business and to the rest of the team.

Count

Each system within your business has its own set of processes, inputs and performance indicators. These days, it's easy to install analytics tools that will help you measure every area of your business. You can be tempted to try to monitor everything, but knowing more does not automatically equate to more value.
This is an area where you want to strengthen your commitment to simplicity. Instead of working to measure every aspect of your business, focus on identifying one key metric within each area of your business to align and scale your systems, processes and virtual team.

Let's consider online stores. They make their money by using websites to sell physical and digital products, but there are dozens of processes which must be engaged to make even one sale.

Store owners hire freelancers to build websites then another set of providers to create content that search engines use to point shoppers to the site. Then someone has to create marketing funnels to control how users experience the site and there has to be a mechanism in place to consistently generate more traffic.

That means someone has to create and place adverts that potential customers want to see. All of these things must happen before the sales pitch is even made and it has to happen on a consistent basis.

While the store owner may have the ability to monitor every aspect of his website it is more effective to monitor the performance of each area of the business by tracking a single KPI.

For example:

- Traffic - Track the number of unique site visitors per week

- Email opt-ins - Track new subscribers to email list for retargeting

- Sales - Track the amount of weekly sales in pounds

- Wow / customer satisfaction - Monitor online feedback, product reviews

- Lifetime - Monitor customer value over the first 12 months

- Viral - Track referrals

By keeping your focus on reaching certain milestones on a weekly basis, and comparing the results week over week, you can keep your team aligned and you can easily spot opportunities for growth.

We have developed our own system to effectively and simply track key metrics in our businesses and those of our clients on a daily, weekly and monthly basis.

Communicate

It is important to keep the lines of communication open within your team. That means making sure you have weekly and monthly team meetings to discuss goals. progress and any concerns. But it also means scheduling time to meet with team members individually.

Your team should have access to you even though they will be having most of their work-related dialogues with your PM. They should have access to you and your PM by email to alert you to situations that may arise and for which they have no immediate fix.

Once a week, have a meeting with your entire team using Skype or GoToMeeting.com. Tip: Gotomeeting has a clearer line and less distortion, important when communicating with team members in locations with poorer internet speeds. Your team needs the consistency of knowing that every seven days they will be able to share their successes and voice their challenges and get directions for how to move forward. You want the consistency of having an official day where you assess your team's collective progress. When I refer to team here I mean your core team that might include on site and remote team members, but only those who are exclusively full time dedicated to work towards your company's mission, not the regular contractors and freelance consultants (designers, developers, researchers, copywriters etc) you work with. You can include them in smaller non regular meetings with other specific team members who are directly concerned with this aspect of your business, like your sales team for example if it is something to do with an event you are planning.

I cannot talk about communicating with a global team without emphasising the importance of making sure your team members have strong, secure Internet connections and multiple methods for staying in contact. Here are some of the tools that we use or have used with our teams at Click Convert Sell and Elite Virtual Team.

COMMUNICATION TOOLS

TYPE OF MEDIA	USAGE	TOOLS
Conference: phone video	**Weekly meetings:** individual team	Skype Google + Hangouts GoToWebinar GoToMeeting
Chat rooms	**Real-time interactive engagement:** post comments give feedbacks ask questions	HipChat Gmail Whatsapp Slack Viber
Written content	**Collaborative:** share documents edit written content enhance from one source	Google Drive Evernote
Shared documents	**Large files instant share without E-mail**	Dropbox WeTransfer

COMMUNICATION TOOLS

TYPE OF MEDIA	USAGE	TOOLS
Remote access:	**Share a computer screen:**	Teamviewer
	allow to access on-site tools and content without having to be on-site	
	computer and server with a remote team member	
Project management software	**Follow project progress:**	Trello Basecamp
	help team members to see a status of a certain task (pending/done)	

Creating a collaborative environment is essential to supporting productivity and creativity. It doesn't matter how superbly qualified and creative your team members are if you do not give them room to share ideas.

Make sharing a habit. Encourage team members to share resources and go through training together when feasible. And lead by example. If you are a solopreneur, you have likely grown accustomed to working for yourself and doing things on your own. It may take some practice before you get to the point where you can consistently offer your team members the right mix of autonomy and supervision. Both are necessary if you want to scale your business.

Once you have found team members that have the technical knowledge and the behavioural competencies to help your organisation grow, trust them with ownership of their segment of your business. Use technology to make it easy for your team to exchange ideas, get help when needed and implement suggestions. In the same way, make it easy for you to see and reward their efforts.

Evaluate

I mentioned earlier that one of the strategies I use in my business is to start base salaries low and increase pay rapidly over the first few months after a new member joins the team. It's a good idea to conduct regularly-scheduled performance reviews every two to three months and establish a reward system where team members receive merit-based pay increases. Put performance reviews on your schedule and on the schedules of your team members and do reviews when you say you will.

I encourage you to conduct one-on-one performance reviews with each member of your team every 90 days. Even with weekly team meetings and the most descriptive and thorough training manuals, team members can get lost in the shuffle. Schedule in a 30-minute Skype session every twelve weeks and use this occasion to review performance, hear and voice any concerns and review compensation when relevant.

Stimulate

It's a good idea to have a scalable way to Wow your customers. Why not also create a way to wow your team? As you identify goals and objectives for your team, include the rewards and bonuses that are up for grabs when you collectively reach your goals.

Incentivise your team to demonstrate to them that your value their contributions.

Your initial response to implementing a rewards program may be resistance. "A rewards and bonuses don't work in my business," you may say. Reverse engineer it and take it apart like we did the quantity surveyor position. I have found a way to create rewards programs that have proven over the past two years to be quite effective in both web-based, remotely-managed businesses and brick and mortar businesses. Rewards work with most things and you can create powerful incentives for your team to help you quickly grow your business if you understand what's important to your team members.

Set goals

Work with your team to set goals - company goals, team goals and individual goals. Once the goals are set, use the job descriptions you created to recruit talent as a checklist to help your team members understand how you will measure their performance. You really don't need a formalised job description for this. The needs assessment you conducted for your business and the skills inventory you created will be sufficient tools to use to provide each team member with a good understanding of which tasks they own and the deliverables you expect to see.

OKR. In the 1970s, Intel President, Andy Grove introduced OKR as an innovative goal-setting system. The system, Objectives and Key Results is a way to connect team members to company goals. We already identified how important the P.A.C mindset is for creating an optimal work environment for your virtual team members. That strategy springs from OKR, the go-to goal-setting system at companies like Google, LinkedIn and Twitter.

Google themselves have credited The OKR system as one of the most important learnings they had and instrumental in aligning their teams with the company goals.

In OKR, the Objective is concrete and aspirational. It should be the key target that if you hit 70% of, would take your business forward to the next level. This then identifies what each team member, department and the business as a whole will do as they all feed down from the key objective. It should be a bold and ambitious goal and it should take effort and time to accomplish.

Key Results are actionable and measurable. They identify how the objectives will be accomplished. They should require effort to achieve, but not be impossible to achieve.

Let's look at the example taught to Google themselves by VC John Doerr. So in the case of an American football team, that John used when presenting the concept to google, the general manager of the football team has the objective to make money for the team owners. His key results are winning the super bowl (or championship) and filling the stands to 88%. Those two key results are then passed down to his head coach and PR team. The key result of winning the Super Bowl becomes the objective of the team coach. The key result of filling the stands to 88% becomes the objective of his PR team. Each of them then passes the key results down onto their team below them thus holding them accountable for specific results that will drive the team towards victory and profitability.

OKR works on three levels - company, team and personal levels. So start by identifying the single biggest company objective for the next 12 months. E.g Achieve Recurring Revenues of £X thousand, or achieve and maintain a 95% customer satisfaction outcome.

This objective is the key plateau you want to break through to a higher level of profitability and productivity.

The key to OKR is making sure everyone on the team and in the company knows the objectives but most importantly the Key Results they are responsible for achieving. Many companies like to keep OKRs visible so that everyone involved in accomplishing these objectives keeps them front-of-mind. As you and your team start completing the tasks needed to accomplish the key results, create a visible representation of the progress that gets updated weekly. In our team we like to use the software Weekdone. For any one objective, once 70% of its results have been achieved, the objective is done.

OKR is an effective method for keeping your team's goals aligned. When everyone knows what needs to be done, they can feel certain about the value of their role in accomplishing each objective. Furthermore, if the results lag behind, you can collectively identify where the problem occurred.

PART FOUR:
Fast, Effective Implementation of Your Outsourcing Game Plan

By now, you have everything you need to leverage outsourcing to scale your business. All that is left is the execution.

Executing The Outsourcing Game Plan yourself

I have been where you are and I know that outsourcing is not easy. It takes time, energy and forethought if you are going to create and implement a strategy to grow your business. Choosing the right virtual team takes requires the same level of deliberation, investigation and depth as hiring on-site employees and the process is equally as challenging. This is not a process you do once and you are done. It is repetitive. Effective, but repetitive.

The best advice I can give you at this point is just to follow the game plan and don't rush it. The Outsourcing Game Plan is not a fast process, but it works. That said, give yourself the time needed to build your systems, recruit your Project Manager and build the rest of your team member by member. Resist the urge to do too much too fast and don't let frustration or impatience rush you into making a quick hire.

You should expect to review dozens of candidates before adding anyone to your team. Be methodical and stay organised. While the process may seem tedious, the returns you will see make the process well worth the investment.

Shortcut the process: Leverage your time by acquiring Elite Virtual Team to streamline the recruiting process

We started using a VA recruited through Elite Virtual Team about three or four months ago. Recruitment of a VA was absolutely stress-free and required minimal work on our side. We simply provided Elite Virtual Team a list of the skills we required and they sourced the appropriate candidates and short-listed three of them for us to interview. The interview was carried out through Skype. We were highly impressed by the high calibre of candidates and their skill sets. All of them were knowledgeable and experienced. We selected one who really stood out in the interview and have now been working with him and he is truly one of our team.

- Kalpesh Bohara, Clinical director at The Dental Suite, Nottingham, United Kingdom.

There are currently between 150 and 200 virtual marketplaces where business owners and busy professionals can recruit talent. Some of the world's best workers are online right now, looking for a company with whom they can invest their talent. So there is no shortage of capable workers. When it comes to recruiting, the heavy lifting is not in identifying which candidates are the most technically proficient;

the work comes in identifying which candidates will be the best fit for your team. And that can be overwhelming.

At Elite Virtual Team, our specialty is being able to find the needle in the haystack. In business, time is money. You have to ask yourself if you really want to spend time learning how to recruit talent, hoping you can find a way to shorten the recruiting process. I would encourage you, however, to entrust your recruiting to our proven system of matching high-value virtual talent from the Philippines with businesses from all over the world.

How EVT works

Our mission is not just to connect you with the right candidate, but to help you in onboarding your new virtual worker so that he or she becomes part of your team. Elite Virtual Team helps you leverage your time by pre-qualifying candidates for you so you don't have to. We review, interview and test dozens of candidates to create a pool of top talent from which you can choose your newest team member.

Once you hire someone from that pool you can start working with them straight away. We provide support for you and the virtual team member for the first week and you will have access to resources like contract templates to help make the onboarding process as seamless as possible. After that, we do not interfere.

Elite Virtual Team charges a one-time initial recruitment fee. We do not collect an ongoing commission. So you do not have to worry about paying inflated monthly fees where the remote worker only sees a portion of what you pay. Your virtual team member gets the full salary you pay. And there are no divided loyalties.

When you hire your full-time team member, our job is done. That person joins your team and is 100% committed to working with you and only with you. We believe that is the best way for you to streamline and grow your business.

There is no rule that says building a team or scaling a business is easy. If it were, every business would do it. Simplicity is the key to controlled growth. Keep your systems simple and easy to understand. Make it easy for them to succeed and make the criteria for measuring their performance straight forward. The days and weeks ahead will be filled with new experiences. There will be challenges, but there will also be successes - many, many successes.

My objective in writing this book was to provide you with a road map to help you drastically shorten your learning curve, and to help you avoid some of the common pitfalls to outsourcing. You can get a wealth of information about how to implement your own outsourcing game plan at www.elitevirtualteam.co.uk.

I wish you all the best in your business endeavour.

Lucie Marchelot Shukla is a parallel entrepreneur and expert on scaling small businesses. Her areas of expertise include, specifically, building virtual teams, creating brands, content marketing and growth accelerator strategies.

Lucie's eye for creative detail and design balances with her logical, structured approach to business. Implementing her powerful combination of talents, Lucie is the Co-Founder and Director of two businesses, Click Convert Sell and Elite Virtual Team and Host of national conference, DominateCon.

She has a BA Honors Degree in Law, and a Merit Graduate Diploma in History of Art and Art-World Practice from Christie's Education. Lucie is driven by her passion for creating exciting brands, world travel, and having a positive impact on the lives of the people she works with.

Keep in touch with Lucie online:

@LucieMShukla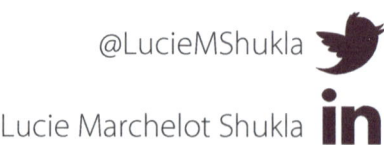

Lucie Marchelot Shukla **in**